CULTIVATING BELONGING IN SCHOOLS

CULTIVATING BELONGING IN SCHOOLS

{ Hannah Wilson }

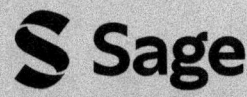

Sage

1 Oliver's Yard
55 City Road
London EC1Y 1SP

2455 Teller Road
Thousand Oaks
California 91320

10th Floor, Emaar Capital Tower
2 MG Road, Sikanderpur, Sector 26
Gurugram, Haryana – 122002
India

8 Marina View Suite 43-053
Asia Square Tower 1
Singapore 018960

Editor: Amy Thornton
Editorial assistant: Harry Dixon
Production editor: Victoria Nicholas
Marketing manager: Lucy Sofroniou
Cover design: Wendy Scott
Typeset by: C&M Digitals (P) Ltd, Chennai, India

© Hannah Wilson 2026

Apart from any fair dealing for the purposes of research, private study, or criticism or review, as permitted under the Copyright, Designs and Patent Act, 1988, this publication may not be reproduced, stored or transmitted in any form, or by any means without the prior permission in writing of the publisher, or in the case of reprographic reproduction, in accordance with the terms of licences issued by the Copyright Licensing Agency. Enquiries concerning reproduction outside those terms should be sent to the publisher.

Library of Congress Control Number: 2025947644

British Library Cataloguing in Publication data

A catalogue record for this book is available from the British Library

ISBN 978-1-0362-0645-1 (pbk)

This book is dedicated to the late, great Karen Giles.
As a lifelong teacher and an Executive Headteacher of two
thriving primary schools in London, Karen was not only a mentor
and a friend, but the epitome of cultivating a culture of belonging
where each and every member of her school community could thrive.
She was a fantastic ambassador for our profession, a role model for
all educational leaders and a brilliant cheerleader of me and my
work. She is missed, but her legacy lives on.

TABLE OF CONTENTS

About this Book — ix
About the Series — xi
About the Author — xiii

Introduction: Why should we care about DEIB? — 1

1 Belonging in Society: How do we develop it? — 9

2 Belonging in Schools: How do we change it? — 27

3 Belonging in the Staffroom: How do we disrupt it? — 45

4 Belonging in the Classroom: How do we foster it? — 63

5 Call to Action: What do we do next? — 81

References — 89
Index — 93

{ ABOUT THIS BOOK }

Teachers and school leaders have been challenged to evaluate whether their classrooms, corridors, playgrounds and curriculum are representative of the communities that they serve. Focusing on students and staff, this book is all about making sure everyone is part of their school community.

- Authored by an expert in the field
- Easy to dip in and out of
- Interactive activities encourage you to write into the book and make it your own
- Fun and engaging illustrations
- Read in an afternoon or take as long as you like with it!

Find out more at
www.sagepub.co.uk/littleguides

ABOUT THE SERIES

A LITTLE GUIDE FOR TEACHERS series is little in size but big on all the support and inspiration you need to navigate your day-to-day life as a teacher.

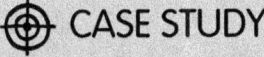 CASE STUDY

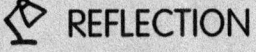 REFLECTION

 RESOURCES

 NOTE IT DOWN

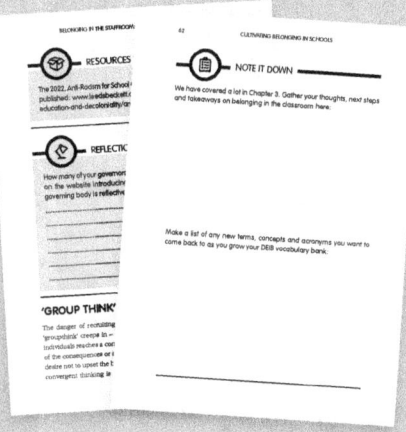

www.sagepub.co.uk/littleguides

ABOUT THE AUTHOR

Hannah Wilson is a Leadership Development consultant, coach and trainer. She is the Co-Founder of #WomenEd and #DiverseEd. She is the Co-Editor of *Diverse Educators: A Manifesto* (Wilson and Kara, 2022) and has contributed to a number of other collective voice books including: #WomenEd's *10% Braver*, Rae Snape's *The Headteacher's Handbook* and Dr Sarah Mullin's *What They Didn't Teach Me on my PGCE*. She is the Director of Belonging Effect (formerly known as Diverse Educators). Hannah previously taught English, Drama and Media Studies over a 20-year career in schools in Kent, London and Oxfordshire. She has held multiple leadership roles including Head of Department, Head of Year, Assistant Headteacher and Deputy Headteacher. She was the founding Headteacher of a start-up secondary school and a founding Executive Headteacher of a start-up primary school. She has also held multiple trust-wide and Teaching School roles including leading Professional Learning and Development, delivering the National Professional Qualifications (NPQ), and leading on the Department for Education's (DfE) Equality and Diversity Fund, along with leading a PGCE and a MA for higher education institutions. Hannah has been a governor and a trustee in multiple settings – she is currently the Chair of a trust board in the Southwest with responsibility for safeguarding. She is also a volunteer mentor for a young carer. She is a connector, a networker and a community-builder so you can find her on LinkedIn or via her websites to continue the conversation.

www.hannah-wilson.co.uk

www.thebelongingeffect.co.uk

INTRODUCTION: WHY SHOULD WE CARE ABOUT DEIB?

LET'S 'START WITH WHY'...

I thought I was quite a good communicator. After all, I had a Degree in Post-Colonial Literature and I had trained as a Teacher of English, Drama and Media Studies. That was until I discovered Simon Sinek's highly regarded book (2011) and TED Talk *Start with Why*. In it he shares the 'Golden Circle' as a model for effective communication – it is a great starting point for any learning journey and for any messaging. So, I am going to use it to break down why I am writing this book and why you are reading it.

SINEK'S GOLDEN CIRCLE

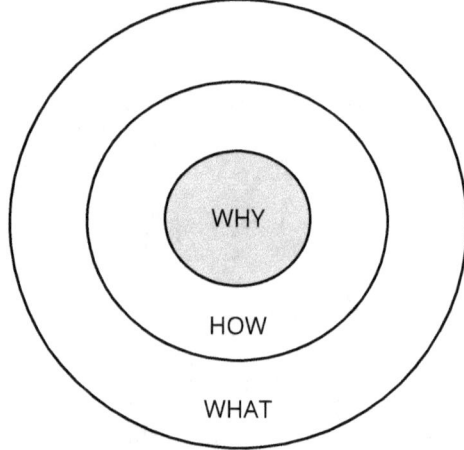

Figure 0.1 Sinek's Golden Circle

If we break down the three circles:

- The 'why' is the hearts and minds, the call to action and the clarifying of the commitment.

- The 'how' is the bringing it to life, the steps we will take and identifying the actions we will make.
- The 'what' is the impact, evaluating the thing we are trying to change and measure.

The key enquiries we will explore over the coming chapters are:

- Why do we need to understand and pay attention to Diversity, Equity, Inclusion and Belonging (DEIB) in education?
- Why does DEIB need to be a 'golden thread' running through every part of school life?
- Why does DEIB need to be everybody's business, in a similar way that safeguarding is?

Whatever role you hold in education and wherever you are doing it, consider the questions:

- Why does your organisation need you to understand DEIB?
- Why do your colleagues need you to better understand DEIB?
- Why do your learners need you to commit to making a difference in the DEIB space?

SO WHY DO I CARE ABOUT DEIB?

I get asked this question a lot. People seem perplexed that I am driven to make our education system more diverse, more equitable and more inclusive. I know what they are thinking: 'but you are white'… 'you are straight'… 'you are cisgender'… 'you do not have a disability'… and all of those things are true of who I am and how I identify.

So, should it matter? Are we saying that only the staff who are multilingual care about our English as an additional language (EAL) learners? That only the staff who have additional needs cater for pupils with special educational needs and disabilities (SEND)? Are we saying that only the staff who experienced socio-economic disadvantage can work on the Pupil Premium (PP) strategy? Of course not, that would be a ridiculous proposition.

So, why do so many teaching staff struggle with understanding why DEIB is important and is everyone's responsibility? From my experience, there are a few key barriers that frequently come up – the lack of confidence, the fear of getting it wrong, the unwillingness to admit a gap in knowledge and the reluctance to relinquish power.

Despite doing this work for over a decade, I also still find it hard to fully articulate as it just feels like the 'right'/'logical'/'commonsense'/ 'values-led'/'human-centred' thing to do. I am aware that each of those descriptors are problematic in their own way, hence the punctuation marks, as they suggest that if you do not understand and embrace DEIB work that you are 'wrong'/'illogical'/'immoral', which is not what I am saying. I am not here to judge you; I am instead here to challenge your thinking and to empower you to take action.

WHAT'S MY STORY?

I was brought up in Devon, in a white majority region. I went to an independent school from 11–16. Growing up, it was the power of reading and the vehicle of travel which exposed me to the realities of the world. I was brought up by young parents, who instilled strong values in my sister and I, who taught us how to advocate for ourselves.

I developed a keen sense of social justice in my mid-teens which led to me reading Post-Colonial Literature at university. I was acutely aware that I did not want to study the canon of dead, white men. I had been inspired by a brilliant teacher at my college who unlocked the feminist in me. This led to me becoming an English teacher, relocating to South London to work in diverse communities to serve in underperforming schools, and my leadership journey started in my second year of teaching as I became a Head of Year and a Head of Subject.

The more senior I became, the more aware I was of the inequalities in our sector. The lack of representation was stark and led to me co-founding grassroots communities including #WomenEd and #DiverseEd to connect people who wanted to make a difference by increasing representation. In 2017 I delivered a TEDx Talk called 'Diverse Dreams'. After juggling my commitment to DEIB as a passion project alongside my day job, when I left headship, I started doing this work full time, just as we went into lockdown and as the world woke up to the stark realities of global social justice.

Ultimately, I have a strong conviction that we have a responsibility for others including how they are treated, and in turn how they are made to feel. I passionately believe that we need people like me, those who hold majority identities to do the work, as allies, advocates and accomplices.

WHY SHOULD YOU CARE ABOUT DEIB?

The world is diverse. UK society is becoming more diverse. Our schools and our classrooms are diversifying rapidly, but our workforce is not. We need a rapid change in how we do things in education when it comes to DEIB. If we keep doing the same – we will keep getting the same.

For some, it is likely that they never saw a teacher, a leader or a governor who looked like them when they were at school. It is also more than possible they did not see themselves in large parts of the curriculum.

Take that in for a second. Imagine how it feels to have your identity consistently affirmed and how it feels to be seen, to be heard and to be valued.

Now imagine how it feels to have your identity forgotten and how that act of exclusion could make you feel – lesson by lesson.

To be clear, I identify as a cisgender, heterosexual, able bodied, christened, white woman. I am not writing this book to finger point, nor to blame and shame. I am writing from the positionality of privilege and power which my identity grants me and from which I have benefitted in multiple ways as a student, as a teacher and as a leader in the education system.

Now, let's pause and consider some provocations of the book's central theme...

Belonging

- A word that everyone uses, but a term that we need to discuss and define in order to understand it, but are we beginning to forget its relationship to diversity, equity and inclusion?
- A buzz word that is being used across the education system, added to school mantras, job adverts are leading with it, but has it become a plaster being used to cover up a bigger problem?
- A bandwagon that people are quickly jumping on, to frame conferences and panels, to write books (the irony!), but are we forgetting about the need to include diverse voices in the dialogue?

SOME OF THE KEY DEFINITIONS

We need to ensure that we are all on the same page when we use the words that are central to this topic.

- D&I
- EDI
- DEI
- DEIB
- DEIJ
- Other combination

Do you know what the letters stand for in the initialism? Do you know what each word means?

Without using a dictionary/device, scribble down on a piece of paper what these words currently mean to you:

- Diversity
- Equality
- Equity

- Inclusion
- Belonging
- Social justice

Were there any that you struggled with? Now go and look them up, chat them through with a friend, a colleague and someone who might have a differing perspective from you.

RESOURCES 0.1

Watch Myers' talk: Diversity is Being Invited to the Party: Inclusion is Being Asked to Dance www.youtube.com/watch?v=9gS2VPUkB3M

Watch Myers' TED talk: How to Overcome our Biases www.ted.com/talks/verna_myers_how_to_overcome_our_biases_walk_boldly_toward_them?language=en

REFLECTION 0.1

What is the difference between diversity and inclusion and how would you define your work or school space with these terms in mind?

What implicit biases exist in your school or workspace? How can you and your colleagues build inclusive spaces?

....

....

(Continued)

Belonging is the feeling that is created as a result of the work we do on DEI. I thus present it as an equation:

Diversity + Equity + Inclusion = Belonging

Why does this book use the word 'cultivating'? I used to talk about building, creating and growing belonging, but for me 'cultivating' captures that there is ongoing work needed and that there are different variables that we need to pay attention to. DEIB is not a 'one and done' approach, belonging takes time and ongoing work in the form of commitment/investment.

So, let's start peeling back the different layers of things to consider when it comes to belonging. And I apologise in advance if you are left with more questions than answers by the end of the book, but that is the nature of the work. It is not a clean nor a linear journey, we will never be done, we will never know it all.

CHAPTER 1
BELONGING IN SOCIETY: HOW DO WE DEVELOP IT?

This chapter covers:

- The landscape
- The law
- The data

AT A CROSSROADS

> *'Community is much more than belonging to something; it's about doing something together that makes belonging matter'.*
> Brian Solis (2014)

> *'Alone we can do so little; together we can do so much'.*
> Hellen Keller (cited in Lash, 1980: 487)

REFLECTION 1.1

Five years ago (in 2020) George Floyd was murdered in the USA.

One year ago (in 2024) the UK experienced race and religion riots during the summer break.

Are we learning from our mistakes when it comes to who belongs and who is marginalised in modern society?

Or are we slipping into a societal crisis where the lack of belonging is leading to anti-social, hateful and dangerous behaviour?

....

....

....

....

....

....

I believe we are at a crossroads and we have a choice to make. Do we continue in the same direction on the well-trodden path, or do we stop and pause, take stock and regroup?

WHAT IS THE THEORY OF BELONGING?

Before considering how we go about cultivating belonging in schools, we should perhaps start with considering what it means to belong as human beings in society – at both an individual and a collective level.

Maslow suggested that the need to belong was a major source of human motivation (Maslow, 1943). It is one of his 'five human needs' along with physiological needs, safety, esteem and self-actualisation. These needs are arranged on a hierarchy and must be satisfied in order.

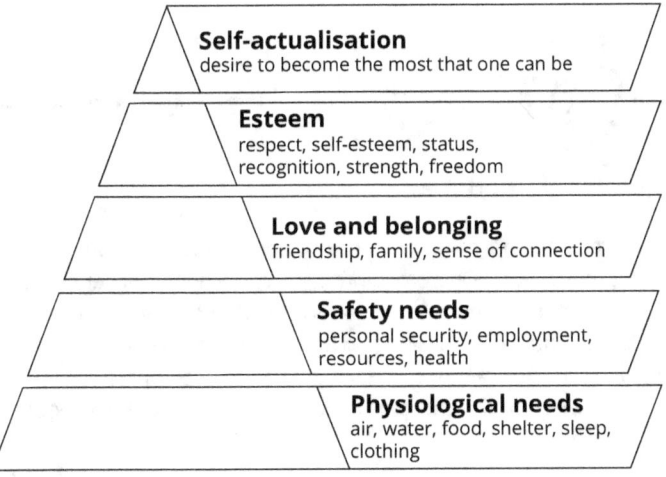

Figure 1.1 Maslow's hierarchy of needs

Take a few minutes to reflect on how your human needs are currently being met. For each of the needs outlined in Figure 1.1, think about what is working and what could improve.

YOUR RELATIONSHIP WITH BELONGING

As you share your reflections it might lead into a deeper, wider conversation about your relationship with belonging. Here are some questions to explore:

- What does it mean to belong?
- How does it feel when we have a strong sense of belonging somewhere?
- What is the impact on us as individuals when we feel included and like 'insiders'/part of the ingroup?
- How does it feel when we do not belong somewhere?
- What is the impact on us as individuals when we feel excluded and like 'outsiders'/part of the outgroup?

CASE STUDY 1.1

Belonging bubble

I often hear that many people have not had to think about these themes before. One brave primary school headteacher broke down in a training session and started crying. She shared that in realising that her belonging had never been challenged, she was oblivious of how it might feel to be othered and excluded, or to exist on the margins. Her belonging bubble had been popped.

THE PSYCHOLOGY OF BELONGING

Kelly-Ann Allen, the founder of the International Belonging Research Laboratory, argues that belonging is the cure for loneliness and isolation (Allen, 2020). It is how we connect with others and how we feel part of a community. Allen emphasises that belonging is a 'fundamental human need' and that the consequences of not experiencing it can be 'devastating'. That if humans cannot find a socially acceptable way to belong, they find belonging in other places, e.g. gangs, cults and radicalised groups.

> 'A sense of belonging in childhood and in adolescence is fundamental to the way we function through our lives.'
> Kelly-Ann Allen (2020: 19)

Consider how many different social groups and communities you belong to. How do these different communities give you a sense of belonging? How do you contribute and how do you receive value from each space?

MEASURING BELONGING

Developed by Hagerty and Patusky in 1995, SOBI or the Sense of Belonging Instrument is a 27-term self-report (Hagerty and Patusky, 1995). It is broken down into SOBI-P, capturing the psychological state of the respondent, and SOBI-A, which focuses on antecedents and how past events shape the current reality for the respondent.

When belonging is disrupted, it impacts our development and our health. The links between belonging and our mental health and wellbeing are thus significant.

RESOURCES 1.1

Watch Dr Nadine Burke-Harris' TED Talk on How Childhood Trauma Affects Health Across a Lifetime: www.ted.com/talks/nadine_burke_harris_how_childhood_trauma_affects_health_across_a_lifetime?language=en

You can also find the Adverse Childhood Experience Questionnaire for Adults freely available from the California Surgeon General's Clinical Advisory Committee: www.acesaware.org/wp-content/uploads/2022/07/ACE-Questionnaire-for-Adults-Identified-English-rev.7.26.22.pdf

THE UK EQUALITY ACT

Published in 2010, the UK Equality Act (Equality Act, 2010) prohibits discrimination, harassment and victimisation based on nine Protected Characteristics:

- Age
- Disability
- Gender reassignment
- Marriage and civil partnership
- Pregnancy and maternity
- Race
- Religion or belief
- Sex
- Sexual orientation

The Equality Act 2010 protects people from discrimination in the workplace and in wider society.

It replaced previous anti-discrimination laws with a single Act, making the law easier to understand and strengthening protection in some situations. It sets out the different ways in which it's unlawful to treat someone. The Act applies to various situations, including work, education, services and public functions.

However, 2010 was a long time ago, and we need an update in who is covered – there are arguments to include additional marginalised identities including menopausal women, neurodivergent people and people who have been displaced, along with a call to update the language being used for some of these identities including the outdated language for gender. In your opinion, who else is missing and should be covered in this law?

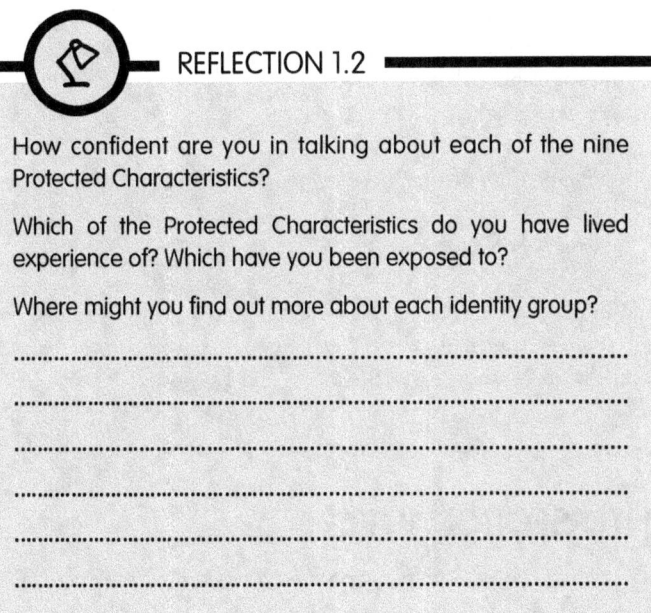

REFLECTION 1.2

How confident are you in talking about each of the nine Protected Characteristics?

Which of the Protected Characteristics do you have lived experience of? Which have you been exposed to?

Where might you find out more about each identity group?

....

....

....

....

....

....

IDENTITY MARKERS

It is important to check in and anchor our identities and our lived experiences. We need to do the work to reflect on who we are, to find the language to describe our experiences, in order to understand ourselves better, but also to reflect on our similarities and differences with others. Our identity is how we see and how we are seen, it is the lens through which we will each explore the ideas in this book.

Spend some time reflecting on your own self-identify and the language you use about yourself by completing your own 'identity map'. To do this, write your name and surround it with all of these other aspects of your identity:

- Age
- Disabilities/additional needs
- Gender identity
- Relationship status
- Parenting status
- Race
- Religion or beliefs
- Sex
- Sexual orientation

Add in other things that are also important to who you are and how you identify, e.g. nationality, first language, citizenship, education, career. Reflect on how easy/hard it is to find the words for each section. Consider which parts of your identity you lead with and readily share and which bits you might not always talk about, and why that might be.

INTERSECTIONALITY

It would be remiss of me at this stage to not bring in the concept of intersectionality and intersectional identities. Our identities are social constructs, and we are all more complex than individual labels may suggest. Assigning labels to individuals and groups can be helpful in places but also harmful at times. Always check and confirm which language people want to be used about them instead of assuming.

Intersectionality is a valuable tool for understanding the complexities of inequality and for developing more effective strategies for social justice. The term was coined by the US academic Kimberlé Crenshaw (Crenshaw, 1989), in the context of analysing workplace discrimination against Black women. Crenshaw used the example of a discrimination case against General Motors, where the court failed to recognise the unique experiences of Black women facing double discrimination due to both their race and gender.

Intersectionality is thus a framework for understanding how various aspects of a person's identity combine to create unique experiences of discrimination and privilege. It recognises that these intersecting identities can lead to overlapping systems of oppression, rather than just additive effects of each individual identity.

> *'If you see inequality as a "them" problem or "unfortunate other" problem, that is a problem.'*
> Kimberlé Crenshaw (1989)

 **CASE STUDY 1.2**

Different shapes, forms and guises

To bring it to life I often use this example. I was a Head of Year for three years at a Boys' High School. The pastoral team were mainly white women, and the students were mainly Global Majority boys, with a high proportion being Black.

(Continued)

> The Black boys in our school experienced the school and the area differently based on the other layers of their identities. If they were Black British, or Black Ghanaian or Black Jamaican their experience differed. If they were Black and straight or Black and gay they were treated differently by their peers. If they were Black and able bodied or Black and neurodivergent they were treated differently by their teachers. If they were Black and Christian or Black and Muslim they belonged to different parts of the local community.

This is where we must be careful with using letters and words to put people into a category. Most people have now rejected BME or BAME in favour of Global Majority but being Black comes in many different shapes, forms and guises so we need to recognise the diversity within the diversity, and be aware of the discrimination within the discrimination.

REFLECTION 1.3

Consider how the intersectionality of your identity has impacted you in your own experience of education and in your career.

....
....
....
....
....
....

We might not call it intersectional data-handling, but when we are filtering attendance, behaviour and attainment data by different demographic fields to analyse trends we are digging into the different layers of identity. For example, we might compare how our white British boys are attending/behaving/attaining against Global Majority boys, we might then add in another filter and look at whether they are EAL or SEND as well. By doing this we realise that some individuals are navigating multiple barriers to successful learning.

RESOURCES 1.2

Watch Crenshaw's talk: The Urgency of Intersectionality www.youtube.com/watch?v=akOe5-UsQ2o

THE UK CENSUS

Every ten years, the Office of National Statistics captures the demographic details of our nation. It gives us a picture of all the people and households and the changing nature of who we are. The last UK Census took place in England, Wales and Northern Ireland in March 2021 (ONS, 2021).

This Census showed us some significant shifts in the diversity of our country. A few headlines:

- **Ethnic diversity:** The proportion of people identifying as being White decreased, while Asian, Asian British or Asian Welsh saw the largest percentage point increase.
- **Languages:** Other than English, Polish was the most common language spoken in England and Wales.

- **Faith:** While Christianity remains the most common religion, its prevalence has decreased, with 'No religion' becoming the second most common response. Less than half the population (46.2%) identified as Christian. Those reporting 'No religion' increased to 37.2%.
- **Sexuality:** The 2021 UK Census revealed that approximately 4.48% of people aged 16 and over who answered the voluntary sexual orientation question identified as lesbian, gay, bisexual, or another sexual orientation (LGB+).
- **Gender identity:** The Census also included a voluntary question on gender identity, with about 0.76% of respondents indicating a gender identity different from their sex registered at birth.

POWER AND PRIVILEGE

In our DEIB training we create a safe space to move from thinking and talking about our own identities and lived experiences, to how our identity gives us power and privilege in different contexts. One of our mantras is *'getting comfortable with being uncomfortable'* and this is when people can begin to squirm as the focus can be quite confronting. We have not all had to consider how each part of our identity has granted us access and opportunities, nor consider how others might be marginalised because they hold a different identity to our own and thereby occupy a different space on the wheel.

The most common diagram to capture this is called 'The Wheel of Power and Privilege', designed by Sylvia Duckworth (Duckworth, 2020) as an adaptation of a model originating from cccrweb.ca. It is a useful conversation starter; however, it is also problematic in how it reduces identity to three all-encompassing sub-categories and some of the language used is quite clumsy.

RESOURCES 1.3

Over time, different variations of the model have been created and the UK Research Integrity Office's 'Academic Wheel of Privilege' is a good example to look at: https://ukrio.org/ukrio-resources/equality-diversity-and-inclusion/academic-wheel-of-privilege

No one likes to be told that privilege has granted them unfair access and opportunities. So, we need to be careful when we are discussing this theme to avoid falling into a deficit model of blaming and shaming. One of my mantras is *'get curious, not critical'* and I try to pose reflections, comments and questions in a way to bring people into the conversation instead of pushing them out and putting them in a defensive space.

Most people define privilege as where they were born, which school they went to and which postcode they live in, more than what they have not experienced. We need to challenge this – I am privileged because I have not experienced racism, ableism, homophobia, islamophobia (and the list goes on). I have not experienced the impact of prejudice nor trauma and I have not navigated the emotional tax of being outed nor othered. I am privileged because most people speak my language and I can access most spaces. I am privileged because I can go on holiday where I like and hold hands with my partner without fear of repercussions.

In Peggy McIntosh's essay, 'White Privilege: Unpacking the Invisible Knapsack' (McIntosh, 2020), she uses the analogy of each of us carrying an invisible knapsack on our backs – mine is relatively light as I am advantaged by invisible privileges and am not weighed down by my identity.

The important part of reflecting on our identities and on our lived experiences is to develop what I have named the '3 Cs': Consciousness, Confidence and Competence. As we become more conscious of who we are, we can become more confident in challenging things around us and we can develop competence in how we show up, stand up and speak out on issues. After all, it does not have to happen to you, to matter to you.

REFLECTION 1.4

As you explore the different models, here are some questions to think or talk about:

- When you place yourself on the wheel what resonates?
- What jars in navigating this model?
- What are you curious about as you look at the different sections and descriptors?
- What are you critical of as you begin to go deeper?
- How might it feel to be on the margins?
- What can you do if you find yourself towards the centre of the wheel?

....

....

....

....

....

....

HATE CRIME

In the UK each March, the Home Office publishes the hate crime data for England and Wales for the prior year. This annual data collection indicates inclusion levels in UK society.

Hate crime is defined as 'any criminal offence which is perceived, by the victim or any other person, to be motivated by hostility or prejudice towards someone based on a personal characteristic':

- Race or ethnicity
- Religion
- Sexual orientation
- Disability
- Transgender identity

For the year ending March 2024, here are some key findings from hate crime data:

- There were 140,561 hate crimes recorded in England and Wales, a 5% decrease compared with the previous year.
- While there was an overall decrease in hate crime, there was a 25% increase in religious hate crimes compared with the previous year. This increase was driven by a rise in hate crimes against Jewish people, and to a lesser extent Muslims, and has occurred since the beginning of the Israel–Hamas conflict.
- As in previous years, the majority of hate crimes were racially motivated, accounting for 7 in 10 of all such offences.
- Transgender hate crimes had been rising before the fall seen in the last year, and now account for 3% of all hate crimes recorded, up from 1% a decade ago (year ending March 2014).

REFLECTION 1.5

What does the hate crime data suggest to us about current levels of belonging in UK society?

Which identity groups are most vulnerable in our country in the current climate?

Do you know anyone who has been a victim of a hate crime?

How were they supported as they navigated this trauma?

....

....

....

....

....

....

'We need to invest in belonging and make it a priority – as a society, financially and through legislation. Belonging is intrinsic to the health, happiness and wellbeing of all people.'
Kelly-Ann Allen (2020: 14)

YOUR COMMUNITY

Here are some questions to help you think through your classroom practice. Consider the diversity of your community:

- How much do you know about the different identities that your learners and their families bring to your area?
- How might you capture and share this information with your pupils to help them develop their understanding of who they are in relation to the wider community?
- How might you contribute to local and regional celebrations and events?
- And when things go wrong, how might you talk about national and regional incidents in an age and stage appropriate way?

RESOURCES 1.4

Watch Thomas' TED talk: Why Representation Really Matters
www.ted.com/talks/aisha_thomas_why_representation_really_matters

SPOTLIGHT ON GOOD PRACTICE

HOPE not hate exists to challenge all kinds of extremism and build local communities. Their strapline is: 'Together, we build HOPE'. https://hopenothate.org.uk/

Citizens UK is a grassroots alliance of local communities and member organisations committed to working together in taking action together for social justice and the common good. https://www.citizensuk.org/

NOTE IT DOWN

We have covered a lot in Chapter 1. Gather your thoughts, next steps and takeaways on belonging in society here before we move on to consider belonging in the school system:

Make a list of any new terms, concepts and acronyms you want to come back to as you grow your DEIB vocabulary bank:

CHAPTER 2
BELONGING IN SCHOOLS: HOW DO WE CHANGE IT?

This chapter covers:

- The school culture
- The vision, mission and values
- The equality policy and equalities objectives

> *'The ache for home lives in all of us, the safe place where we can go as we are and not be questioned.'*
> Maya Angelou (1987: 196)

And we find ourselves at school a lot! As a student from 4–18, or as an educator in our adult lives, we spend a large proportion of our time in schools, so we need to make sure that they are places of inclusion and spaces for belonging.

One of the problems we face is that every teacher, leader and governor likes to consider themselves as being inclusive. When I am running training, I often share the provocative invitation: put your hand up if your school is inclusive (all hands go up) and keep your hands up if you are inclusive (all hands stay up). My point is to get people thinking about how to move from intention to impact. We might think we are inclusive, but what are we doing to proactively include others? And more importantly, who are we actively including? By contrast, who may we be inadvertently excluding?

DESIGNING FOR INCLUSION, LEADING WITH DIVERSITY

One of the approaches I have developed over time is to design for inclusion and lead with diversity, instead of waiting for difference to announce itself (as more often than not people do not want to single themselves out and will suffer in silence).

Let me give you a few examples:

1. You are inviting candidates to interview – do you wait for someone to ring up to disclose that they need a private place to express their milk or access to a prayer space or do we include that in the invite to all candidates to truly embody our

commitment to DEIB? Do you send out the questions in advance to all candidates or do you wait for someone to share that they are neurodivergent and need additional processing time?

2. You are hosting an event at your school – do you consider who might need access to a disabled parking space and the lift in advance? Do you plan for which toilets everyone will use or ensure that your menu is diverse and inclusive? Or do you wait for someone to email and say, 'Hi, I only eat Halal meat, will I be catered for?' or 'Hi, I am non-binary, will there be gender neutral toilets available?'.

If we are truly inclusive and we really want to help people to feel like they belong in our school, then we design DEIB into the activity, event, trip or opportunity, instead of centring the majority we find and remove the barriers in advance.

SCHOOL CULTURE

School culture encompasses the shared values, beliefs and practices that shape a school's atmosphere and influence how people interact within it. It's essentially the personality of the school, dictating norms, expectations, and the overall experience for students, teachers and staff.

Key aspects of school culture include:

- Shared values and beliefs
- Norms and expectations
- Traditions and rituals
- Relationships and interactions
- Leadership style
- Learning environment
- Community involvement

A healthy and inclusive culture is vital for all stakeholders to flourish and thrive as it leads to:

- Student success
- Teacher wellbeing
- School improvement
- School climate

Culture is a concept that encompasses the social behaviour, institutions and norms found in human societies, as well as the knowledge, beliefs, arts, laws, customs, capabilities, attitudes and habits of the individuals in these groups.

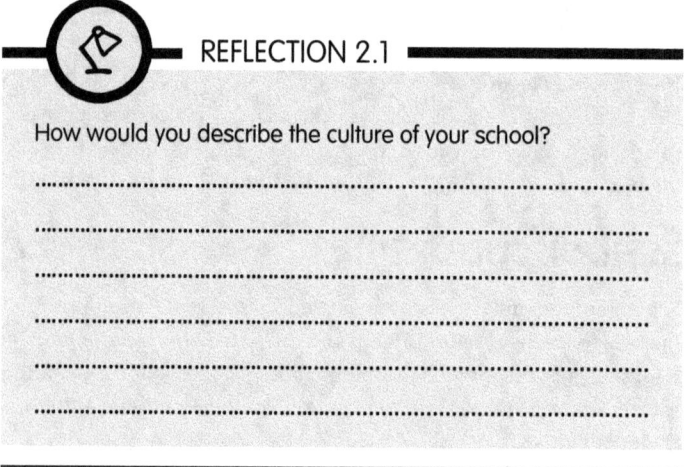

REFLECTION 2.1

How would you describe the culture of your school?

....
....
....
....
....
....

VISION, MISSION AND VALUES

A school's culture is framed by the storytelling around and about the school. When I began teaching in 2002, schools might have had some aims, but they did not clearly lay out who they were in a consistent way. Since then, we have seen a concerted effort to explicitly articulate and thereby differentiate what schools stands for.

Your vision:

- Your overarching aspiration of what you hope to achieve or to become.

- A broad description of the value you can provide.
- The visual image of what you are trying to produce or become.
- Your vision will inspire people and motivate them to want to be part of and contribute to your team.

Your mission:

- Describing what you need to do now to achieve the vision.
- Your vision supports your mission, but your mission is more specific.
- It defines how you are different from other individuals.
- Your mission is more actionable than your vision.
- Your mission leads to strategic goals.

Your values:

- Form your code of ethics, defining what you believe in.
- Establish how you behave and interact with others.
- Provide a moral direction to guide decision making and establish a protocol for actions.

CASE STUDY 2.1

Consistency and clarity in school culture

I once worked for a formidable Headteacher. He was fierce, but fair, always honest, even brutal at times. He was a straight-talking, old-school leader but you always knew where you stood with him. His mantra was simple: 'Give respect, get respect'. This was drummed into the pupils at our turnaround school. I distinctly remember a group of confident Year 11 boys taking him on and calling out the hypocrisy of how this value was being embodied. They asked him, directly, 'How is it respectful

(Continued)

for the students to line up to get their lunch in the dining hall, and for the staff to jump the queue and cut in?'. He slept on it and announced in our staff briefing the next day that staff would now need to line up and wait their turn. He recognised that some behaviours were undermining the value of respect. There was some fallout. Not all staff agreed that they should be embodying respect in this way.

I share this memory with you, as we often find inconsistencies and contradictions between what we say and what we do. Culture is built on consistency, and consistency comes from clarity but also accountability. The clearer we are on what we say, what we expect, the more consistent we become in what we do.

Curriculum expert Mary Myatt's often-quoted phrase 'values lived, not laminated' (Myatt, 2017) chimes with me and my experience of values sometimes being painted in beautiful colours across walls and splashed across websites, but when you scratch the surface, the values are being instilled in the pupils but not modelled by the adults in the school.

 REFLECTION 2.2

- What are your school values?
- How consistently are they being modelled?
- How do they relate to your personal values?
- How do the school values speak to a commitment of DEIB?

[lined note-taking area]

THE BRITISH VALUES

As defined by the UK government, the British Values (formerly referred to as the 'Fundamental' British Values) are democracy, the rule of law, individual liberty, and mutual respect and tolerance of those with different faiths and beliefs. These values are considered fundamental to life in modern Britain and are promoted in schools and other settings.

Here's a breakdown of each value:

- **Democracy:** This encompasses the right to vote, participate in decision-making processes, and have one's voice heard within a framework of law and order.
- **Rule of law:** This emphasises the importance of laws and regulations that apply equally to everyone, ensuring a fair and just society.
- **Individual liberty:** This refers to the freedom to make choices, express opinions and live one's life within the boundaries of the law, while also respecting the rights of others.
- **Mutual respect and tolerance of different faiths and beliefs:** This highlights the importance of respecting the diverse beliefs, cultures and backgrounds of all individuals, regardless of their faith or lack thereof.

It is important to note that these values are not unique to Britain but are considered essential for a harmonious and inclusive society. They are often integrated into educational settings through the curriculum, school activities, and discussions about citizenship and social responsibility.

> **REFLECTION 2.3**
>
> - How do the British Values show up in your school?
> - How are they talked about and presented through displays, assemblies and the wider curriculum?
> - Did you know that the 'Fundamental' British Values were originally introduced as part of the Prevent Strategy to support the Government's counter-terrorism strategy?
> - What are the potential tensions in the delivery of the British Values in your setting's context?
> - Does this awareness now change the lens through which we consider belonging in our setting?
>
> ....
> ....
> ....
> ....
> ....
> ....

EQUALITY POLICY

A school equality policy aims to ensure all members of the school community are treated fairly and have equal opportunities, regardless of their background or Protected Characteristics. This includes preventing discrimination, harassment and victimisation, as well as promoting inclusion and good relations among all students and staff. The policy should ensure that all members of the school community are aware of their responsibilities and rights when it comes to DEIB.

EQUALITIES OBJECTIVES

School equality objectives aim to eliminate discrimination, advance equal opportunities, and foster positive relationships among all students and staff. These objectives are typically aligned with the Equality Act 2010 and focus on creating an inclusive environment where everyone feels valued and respected. Schools should establish clear equality objectives, which are specific, measurable, achievable, relevant and time-bound (SMART). These objectives should be regularly reviewed and updated to ensure they are effective.

REFLECTION 2.4

- When was the last time you read your school's equality policy?
- Who is responsible for it and when is it next due to be updated?
- Are you familiar with your school's equalities objectives?
- Which identities from the nine Protected Characteristics (Equality Act, 2010) do they focus on?
- Who is responsible for them and when are they next due to be updated?
- Is there anything you can identify that is missing and that needs including in either document?

(Continued)

PREJUDICE LOGS

Historically, schools had to log all racist and homophobic incidents and report them to their governors and to their Local Authority. Different schools logged such incidents in different ways, sometimes manually but nowadays more often as not electronically. Sometimes these incidents are logged on a behaviour system and other times they are added on a safeguarding system. Often this data is inconsistent and contradicts itself regarding the number of each type of incident and the follow up consequences and interventions.

CASE STUDY 2.2

Specific incident tracking

As a Headteacher and Designated Safeguarding Lead (DSL), we introduced CPOMs as our software for logging all behavioural, safeguarding and discrimination. We manually added all of the Protected Characteristics into the drop-down options so we

> could accurately track patterns in behaviour. We could also then review the curriculum to proactively identify gaps to close in the staff's teaching and the students' learning. Moreover, we could reactively target year groups and smaller groups of students (and parents) who needed follow-up support.

COMMUNICATION

I have seen a range of approaches to school culture. Schools' vision, mission and values do not vary that much, nor do their interpretation of the British Values, but how they manifest as cultural expectations and behaviours can look and feel very different in different contexts. For me some of the keys to a strong, positive culture where people can belong are:

- Clear, open and honest communication
- Focus on investing in relational capital
- Willingness to engage in courageous conversations
- Commitment to creating psychological safety

AN 'OPEN DOOR' POLICY

Many school leaders will talk about their commitment to listening through them holding an 'open door' policy where anyone can come and talk to them, any time about anything. This sounds great in theory, but I am curious about who accepts this invitation and crosses the threshold to share an unwelcome truth or an unpopular opinion. For some identities this would be a dangerous thing to do as it would put them in a vulnerable position and it might perpetuate a harmful stereotype about one of the identity groups they belong to. Is there another way that leaders can be accessible to listen to the views of staff?

REFLECTION 2.5

A great way to gather feedback on our DEIB approaches is via staff, student and parent voice. Think about the opportunities your school provides for stakeholders to share their views.

- What activities happen and how frequently (e.g. an annual survey, a termly focus group)?
- Are there specific questions in these voice activities about DEIB?
- How and when are the results shared with the wider staff to be able to learn from these insights?

....
....
....
....
....
....

COURAGEOUS CONVERSATIONS

In courageous conversations, whether in the context of performance appraisal, mentoring or coaching, individuals are encouraged to express their views openly and truthfully, rather than defensively or with the purpose of laying blame. Integral to courageous conversations is an openness to learn.

Typical examples include handling conflict, confronting a colleague, expressing an unpopular idea on a team, asking for a favour, saying no to a request for a favour, asking for a salary raise, or trying to have a conversation with someone who is avoiding you.

Some great books that I have built into my training on this theme are: *Radical Candor* by Kim Scott (2017), *Fierce Conversations* by Susan Scott (2002) and *Daring Greatly* by Brené Brown (2012). I particularly like the 'Care-Challenge' matrix from Kim Scott which explores the different cultures we create when one of these elements is missing. I recommend you check it out.

CASE STUDY 2.3

The 'Polish' corner

When I moved from being an Assistant Headteacher in one school to being a Deputy Headteacher in our sister school, the demographic of our school community changed vastly despite being only a few miles apart in South London. I went from working in a school with a Black majority intake to a school with a White Other majority. I line-managed EAL which was a whole school priority as we had 37 languages recorded on the Census. I found the EAL centre tucked away on the 3rd floor, so we moved it to the old staffroom which was in the centre of the school, re-naming it as The Language Centre (TLC for short). The second most common language spoken in our school was Polish. To my discomfort, there was a place in the playground called 'The Polish Corner'. I initiated a courageous conversation with my leadership colleagues to unpack this.

> **REFLECTION 2.6**
>
> Do you have any areas in your school 'owned' by a particular group of staff or students? How does this make you feel? What does this suggest to you about their sense of belonging? How might you get curious about this with others?
>
> ....
> ....
> ....
> ....
> ....
> ....

PSYCHOLOGICAL SAFETY

Psychological safety, a concept popularised by Professor Amy Edmondson (Edmondson, 2018), refers to a team environment where individuals feel safe to take interpersonal risks, such as speaking up with ideas, questions, concerns or mistakes, without fear of negative consequences. It's the belief that one won't be punished or humiliated for being candid. Edmondson's work highlights that psychological safety is a crucial ingredient for high-performing teams and resilient organisations, fostering innovation, learning and growth.

Key aspects of psychological safety are:

- Interpersonal risk-taking
- Candor and openness

- Learning and innovation
- Reduced fear
- Shared belief

The impacts of increased psychological safety include:

- Improved team performance
- Increased innovation
- Reduced errors
- Enhanced learning
- Stronger organisational culture

RESOURCES 2.1

Education Support, a UK charity supporting the wellbeing of educators, have created a school version of Edmondson's Psychological Safety audit which is downloadable from their website: www.educationsupport.org.uk/resources/for-organisations/guides/psychological-safety-audit/

REFLECTION 2.7

How psychologically safe is your classroom and how do you know? Consider how you get feedback from your students, their parents, your line manager and your peers. Is there a way of building-in a focus on psychological safety and what is working/ what could be improved? How might this benefit your learners?

(Continued)

SPOTLIGHT ON GOOD PRACTICE

Cities of Sanctuary – from community groups to councils, schools to libraries, these vibrant networks provide welcome, support and opportunity to people seeking sanctuary. Find out more here: https://cityofsanctuary.org/

Schools of Sanctuary – schools that educate the whole school community about the experiences and realities of people who have been forced to flee their homes/country, to foster understanding, connection and solidarity. Find out more here: https://schools.cityofsanctuary.org/

# NOTE IT DOWN

We have covered a lot in Chapter 2. Gather your thoughts, next steps and takeaways on belonging in schools here:

Make a list of any new terms, concepts and acronyms you want to come back to as you grow your DEIB vocabulary bank:

CHAPTER 3
BELONGING IN THE STAFFROOM: HOW DO WE DISRUPT IT?

This chapter covers:

- **Belonging in the workplace**
- **The diversity of ITTE and governance**
- **The Talent Pipeline**

> *'Because true belonging only happens when we present our authentic, imperfect selves to the world, our sense of belonging can never be greater than our level of self-acceptance.'*
> Brené Brown (2012: 122)

This chapter explores staff experience of belonging as an adult in the school system and specifically in the staffroom. Belonging is not just for our young people – all school stakeholders need to belong. Some questions to consider:

- Who gets to become a teacher and to progress as a leader?
- What do we need to do differently to increase opportunity, access and representation within our sector?
- Who gets to belong in the staffroom?
- How can schools ensure that their staff also have a high sense of belonging within their community?

BELONGING: THE KEY TO HIGH PERFORMING TEAMS

Owen Eastwood (2022) has become a notable voice on this topic – his central thesis is that as humans, we need to feel like we belong and we respond significantly to a sense of shared identity. Conversely, we react badly to being treated like outsiders or being in groups of people that we don't trust or don't feel trusted by.

Owen emphasises that belonging isn't a 'nice to have'; it's essential. It reduces anxiety, builds confidence and fosters resilience. When individuals feel they truly belong, their stress decreases, motivation rises and performance improves.

PROFESSIONAL IDENTITY

In *Pride and Progress: Making Schools LGBT+ Inclusive Spaces* (2023), Dr Adam Brett and Jo Brassington share an activity for us to explore the different spheres of our identity as we become teachers and visible role models in our schools, staffrooms and classrooms.

Draw three overlapping circles like a 3-way Venn diagram. Label the three circles:

- Personal identity (home you)
- Teacher identity (classroom you)
- Colleague identity (staffroom you)

Annotate the diagram to capture who you are currently showing up as in each space. Consider the overlaps between these three layers of your identity. Are there choices you are making about which bits of your identity you reveal to who? Are there aspects of who you are and your story that are less visible and that you want to make more explicit?

PROFESSIONAL BELONGING

Take time to think about what belonging means to you. Can you finish the sentence *When I experience belonging …?*

Here are some endings that often come up:

- I feel heard
- I feel needed
- I feel present
- I feel supported
- I feel accepted
- I feel involved
- I feel invited

- I feel welcomed
- I feel safe
- I feel known
- I feel trusted

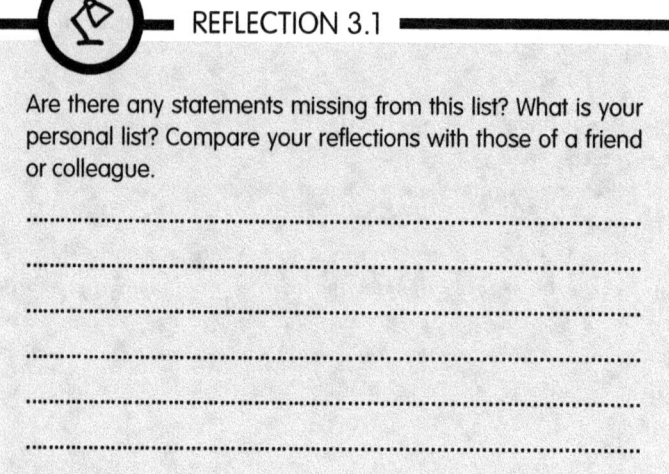

Are there any statements missing from this list? What is your personal list? Compare your reflections with those of a friend or colleague.

....
....
....
....
....
....

WORKFORCE DATA

When we look demographically at UK teachers, the 2021 statistics are telling:

- 85% of UK teachers were from white British backgrounds, as were 92.5% of Headteachers.
- 75.5% of UK teachers were women.

How does this data compare to your school's workforce breakdown?

As a white woman in education I have always been in the majority, I have been represented. However, the more senior I became the less role models I had around me and above me which is why I co-founded #WomenEd a decade ago.

A SHADOW OVER THE SYSTEM

Section 28 was a law introduced in 1988 that prohibited local authorities from intentionally promoting homosexuality or publishing material with the intention of promoting homosexuality. It prevented schools from teaching that homosexuality is a valid family relationship. It restricted people working in health and education until 2003 when it was repealed, although clear guidance about what is expected has never been published.

It is important to be mindful of how many of your school community's parents and carers were at school during this time, as they may be unaware that the law has changed and think we are breaking the law by validating the existence of LGBT+ people and families. Furthermore, it is estimated that 8% of the teacher workforce identify as LGBT+, although the Census will report the more conservative figure of 3%, as there is a fear, even in 2025, of disclosing.

'USUALISING' DIVERSITY

Sue Sanders coined the phrase 'usualising' as an alternative to 'normalising' (Fenwick and Sanders, 2012). Sanders encourages us to usualise diversity as a way of visibilising marginalised identities.

RESOURCES 3.1

Watch Dr Sue Sanders' TED Talk 'Visibilising and Usualising' the LGBTQ+ Community': www.youtube.com/watch?v=QfY4AZLvx4M

DEIB RESEARCH

Data from Edurio (2021) and NFER (2024) reveals that the representation of non-white educators, disabled individuals and LGBTQIA+ educators remains low in leadership positions. Addressing these disparities calls for thoughtful recruitment, retention and career development strategies.

For many educators, especially those from marginalised groups, remaining in the profession long term can be tough. Research from BERA (Stones and Glazzard, 2019) on LGBTQIA+ teachers and the 'Missing Mothers' project (2024) highlights how workplace culture, lack of support and discrimination can push talented educators away.

REFLECTION 3.2

Consider your own experience as an adult in the sector. As you navigated further and higher education, what did you notice about levels of diversity in the spaces you occupied? If you trained to teach, what did you observe about your peers and your mentors? Did you notice a difference between who was teaching and who was learning? As you have established yourself in your career, if you look up the leadership ladder in your setting, who do you see above you on the senior leadership team (SLT) and governing body?

....

....

....

....

....

....

THE 'PERCEPTION GAP'

Edurio's 2021 EDI report identifies a perception gap between the experience of leaders in a school and staff in a school when it comes to DEIB. Governors and senior leaders setting the vision and strategy for the school often hold a majority identity. They can be guilty of assuming that their experience of the school reflects the wider staff's experience.

> 'When you start paying attention to diversity, you notice it (and notice its absence!). And based on the culture of your upbringing and the culture of your organization, you may or may not be primed to think consciously about innovation.'
> David Livermore (2009: 236)

DEIB AND ITTE

A lot of data has been recorded over the last few years on who is entering the profession at Initial Teacher Training in Education (ITTE). The research also looks at who is applying and not successfully securing a place in ITTE. Yes, we are in a recruitment crisis, but we are also in a retention crisis. Attrition rates in our sector are high – especially those leaving after three and five years. In 2022, a group of academics collaborated on the Anti-Racism in ITTE Framework: www.ncl.ac.uk/social-science/research/anti-racism-framework/

NFER RESEARCH

Commissioned by Mission 44, the 2024 'Ethnic diversity in the teaching workforce: evidence review', 'identifies the barriers and promising approaches to support recruitment, retention and progression of people of colour within the teaching workforce' (NFER, 2024).

Key findings:

- People of colour are less likely to receive and accept an offer for Initial Teacher Training (ITT) compared with their white peers. Negative experiences during ITT help to explain why fewer trainee teachers of colour achieve qualified teacher status (QTS).
- Teacher retention is lower for teachers of colour than for their white counterparts. Beyond high workload, key reasons for leaving include (1) overt and covert racial discrimination; (2) disillusionment with their ability to make a difference for pupils from ethnic minority backgrounds; and (3) lack of progression opportunities.
- Barriers to recruitment, retention and progression coalesce around the unequal treatment of teachers of colour in a system that was not designed to support either ethnic or intersectional diversity. An anti-racist school culture is a key enabler of progression. (NFER, 2024)

Commissioned again and funded by Mission 44, the 2025 report, 'Ethnic disparities in entry to teacher training, teacher retention and progression to leadership', finds that equalising the disparities in progression between applicants and teachers of different ethnic groups would significantly contribute to the Government's goal of recruiting 6,500 new teachers (NFER, 2025). It follows NFER's previous research on racial equality in the teacher workforce to further explore the factors influencing ethnic disparities at three key progression points: entry into ITT, progression to leadership and retention.

Key findings:

- There are significant ethnic disparities in postgraduate ITT rejection rates among UK-domiciled applicants that are not explained by differences in applicant and application characteristics. The available data suggests that discrimination by ethnic background is likely to play a role, although we cannot definitively rule out other factors (such as differences in qualification levels or work experience).

- Teachers from Asian and Black ethnic backgrounds have a significantly higher intention to apply for promotion than their white counterparts. This suggests that the disparities in progression rates found in our previous research were not due to a lack of interest among ethnic minority teachers and more likely to reflect a lack of opportunity or inequitable treatment in decision-making processes.
- Teachers from a Black ethnic background were more likely than their white counterparts to report experiencing bullying and harassment, that they did not feel valued by their school and that a lack of support from superiors was an important reason for considering leaving. These are likely drivers for the finding that teachers from a Black ethnic background are more likely to consider leaving state-sector teaching than their white counterparts. (NFER, 2025)

CASE STUDY 3.1

The importance of staff awareness

We worked with a School-based Initial Teacher Training (SCITT) in the South of England for three years. At inspection, Ofsted gave them glowing feedback about the trainee teachers' awareness of their legal responsibilities and their clear moral imperative for embedding their commitment in their teaching. A few months later the lead school in their Multi-Academy Trust (MAT) was also inspected. They dropped three inspection grades as the pupils highlighted that staff were not equipped to deal with the prejudice being reported to them by the students, so the school was not safe.

> *'Belonging is when you feel safe and valued for embracing what makes you different.'*
> Liz Fosslien (Fosslien and West Duffy, 2019: 8)

RESOURCES 3.2

Emily Meadows is an LGBTQ+ consultant for schools. Her 'You Belong Here' posters (range of languages) are available for download and display: www.emilymeadows.org/blog/u5omunfssmmx5jork7ikt9uf5lltuc

DEIB AND THE TALENT PIPELINE

Reviewing who we recruit, who we develop and who we retain is an important part of our people management strategy. We should know the breakdown of diversity data at every rung of the ladder. We need to support existing leaders in progressing, but we also need to be investing in aspiring leaders.

DEIB AND GOVERNANCE

The UK school system is unique with the power it gives volunteers to govern our schools, colleges and trusts, but there is an opportunity to review who sits on our boards, what diversity they bring to the table and how they represent our communities.

RESOURCES 3.3

In 2022, the Anti-Racism for School Governance framework was published: www.leedsbeckett.ac.uk/research/centre-for-race-education-and-decoloniality/anti-racism-for-school-governors/

REFLECTION 3.3

How many of your governors have you met? Is there information on the website introducing them all? Do you feel that your governing body is reflective of your school community?

....
....
....
....
....
....

'GROUP THINK' AND 'REBEL IDEAS'

The danger of recruiting and promoting homogenous groups is that 'group think' creeps in – a phenomenon that occurs when a group of individuals reaches a consensus without critical reasoning or evaluation of the consequences or alternatives. Group think is based on a common desire not to upset the balance of a group of people. The alternative to convergent thinking is divergent thinking. 'Rebel ideas' challenge the status quo and embrace diverse perspectives to foster innovation and better decision-making. Matthew Syed (2019) explores this concept in his book of the same name, emphasising the power of cognitive diversity – different ways of thinking and approaching problems – in overcoming challenges and achieving breakthroughs.

THE GEC'S 26,000 VOICES REPORT

Dr Nic Ponsford, founder of the Global Equality Collective (GEC), has spent the last few years collating data about staff and students' experiences of school life. Here are some key findings from their research into how safe, seen or supported staff feel in school (Global Equality Collective, 2025):

- 60% of staff feel they can be their authentic selves at work.
- 62% of parent/carer staff feel excluded due to caregiving responsibilities.
- 46% of staff feel represented in school leadership.
- 41% of staff with mental health or neurodivergent needs do not feel safe reporting issues.
- 40% of staff say they need flexible working–or will consider leaving.

REFLECTION 3.4

How might this national data compare to your school's data?

IDEAS FOR YOUR STAFFROOM

Ask your team, or group of staff some key questions:

1. How **safe** do you feel in our staffroom?
2. How **included** do you feel in our staff body?
3. How **represented** do you feel in our leadership team?
4. How **diverse** are the role models that you have been exposed to during training?
5. How do staff events support your sense of **belonging**?
6. How **equitably** are opportunities for development and promotion allocated?
7. Is there anything else you would like to tell me about your experience of our school?

STAFF DEIB SURVEYS

Staff DEIB surveys are tricky. Some staff will not feel psychologically safe enough to be open and honest in their answers. Some staff will have been asked to share their thoughts in the past and nothing may have changed.

Be careful about DEIB surveys that go out cold, with no context and no staff session to explain what is being asked and why. Be clear on how the data will be handled and stored.

BELONGING IN THE WORKPLACE

Dr Nilufar Ahmed, an academic with EDI responsibility at Bristol University, wrote a piece for *The Conversation* exploring this theme (Ahmed, 2024). In it she states:

> Many employers know the value of belonging, boasting that their organisation is like a family – a place where everyone is welcome and takes care of each other. But in reality, just being hired isn't necessarily enough to feel like you belong.

> Belonging is about feeling accepted and included. This might mean feeling 'seen' by your colleagues and manager, and that your work is recognised, rewarded and respected.

She goes on to outline that belonging is good for business. DEIB makes organisations more productive and more profitable. Diverse teams that are inclusive and have a deep commitment to belonging outshine homogenous teams in multiple ways.

More importantly, belonging and being included supports workplace retention, reduces loneliness and sick days. People leave jobs to find better connections and a community they are more values-aligned with. Moreover, the next generation of employees places DEIB high up their search list for what they are looking for in a prospective employer.

Let's be clear, better staff belonging in a school leads to better pupil belonging. Better pupil belonging leads to improved attendance, increased engagement and enhanced outcomes. Belonging leads to better health and better results for all, especially our young people in preparing them for their futures.

> *'To me, belonging creates magic. It means creating a culture of trust, where all voices are heard, and where people feel safe bringing their authentic selves to work. When employees feel like they belong, when they know that they can be themselves, they unlock what makes them great.'*
> Pat Wadors (LinkedIn Talent Solutions, 2016)

CASE STUDY 3.2

The Equality and Diversity Fund

I spent a year leading Professional Learning and Development in a large MAT in London. At that time the DfE was investing in the school workforce through the Equality and Diversity Fund. Our MAT had two teaching schools so we were able to apply for two grants, so we focused one pipeline project on women in leadership and another on the global majority pipeline. The funding enabled us to offer training, coaching/mentoring and networking opportunities to aspirant leaders from a marginalised identity. Leading this initiative is one of my career highlights, and ten years on it is fantastic to see where these leaders now are in their careers.

LEADING WITH CULTURAL INTELLIGENCE

As a trainer with a passion for DEIB, I was delighted when I discovered the Cultural Intelligence Center in the US and their Cultural Intelligence (CQ) framework.

CQ is the ability to relate and work effectively with people from different cultural backgrounds. It encompasses understanding cultural differences, adapting behaviour, and adjusting strategies to navigate diverse cultural contexts. Developing CQ is crucial in today's globalised and diverse world, enabling individuals to thrive in multicultural settings and enhance their performance in both professional and interpersonal contexts.

RESOURCES 3.4

The Cultural Intelligence Center's four-part process helps leaders create a cyclical strategy for evolving their commitment to DEIB:

1. Drive
2. Knowledge
3. Strategy
4. Action

Find out more here: https://culturalq.com/about-cultural-intelligence/global-cq/

REFLECTION 3.5

How might this CQ model help you and your team/leaders/governors in shaping your DEIB strategy and creating momentum?

....

....

....

....

....

....

SPOTLIGHT ON GOOD PRACTICE

Pride and Progress are a podcast, platform and community group amplifying the voices of LGBT+ educators and exploring ways to collectively reimagine our educational spaces as more LGBT+ inclusive. They believe in a holistic approach to DEIB so that every person in a school community can feel free to be themselves, feel safe, feel seen, feel supported and feel like they belong. www.prideprogress.co.uk/

Aspiring Headteachers is a social enterprise dedicated to breaking down racial barriers in education in the UK. Their goal is to increase representation of Black teachers and educators in school leadership, ultimately creating a better learning environment for all children. www.aspiringheads.com/

# NOTE IT DOWN

We have covered a lot in Chapter 3. Gather your thoughts, next steps and takeaways on belonging in the classroom here:

Make a list of any new terms, concepts and acronyms you want to come back to as you grow your DEIB vocabulary bank:

CHAPTER 4
BELONGING IN THE CLASSROOM: HOW DO WE FOSTER IT?

This chapter covers:

- The data
- The research
- The identity-affirming classroom

> 'Belonging happens when people have ownership of what happens in a space. Belonging means a person knows their voice is heard, they have agency, they believe that if they are not there in that space, people will sense that something is missing'.
> Suzy Kaback (2025)

This chapter explores the experience of belonging that your learners have in your classroom. Some questions to get us started:

- Why do we need our pupils to experience belonging?
- Who gets to authentically belong in the modern-day classroom?
- How are we currently creating belonging?
- What do we need to do differently in order to design classrooms that enable more learners to be seen, to be heard, to feel safe?

DIVERSITY IN THE CLASSROOM

Consider the diversity of your classroom. How much do you know about the identity of your learners? There are multiple data sets you can draw on to inform you. Consider the quantitative and qualitative cycles of gathering and sharing data to inform you about diversity levels.

Pick a class and complete the following worksheet (if you cannot readily find the data, then consider who you could ask to help you).

Worksheet 4.1 The diversity of your classroom

Identity marker	My class's data	What do I need to affirm in my teaching to create belonging for this group of students?	What barriers do I need to find and remove for these learners to enable them to be successful in my classroom?
Sex (e.g. male/female/intersex)			
Race (e.g. Black/brown/white)			
Religion (e.g. their faith)			
Gender (e.g. cisgender/non-binary/transgender)			
Sexuality (e.g. LGBTQ+)			

(Continued)

Worksheet 4.1 (Continued)

Identity marker	My class's data	What do I need to affirm in my teaching to create belonging for this group of students?	What barriers do I need to find and remove for these learners to enable them to be successful in my classroom?
SEND (e.g. physical/hidden disabilities, neurodiversity)			
Multilingualism (e.g. EAL/English is not their first/home language)			
Mental health and wellbeing (e.g. anxiety, self-harming)			
Socio-economic disadvantage (e.g. they might be PP/FSM)			

CONNECTED BELONGING

'Connected Belonging: A relational and identity-based approach to schools' role in promoting child wellbeing' is a research project from academics Ceri Brown, Alison Douthwaite and Michael Donnelly (2025). They have built on the foundations established by Allen et al.

(2021) who identified four components underpinning the notion of belonging: competencies, opportunities, motivations and perceptions.

The 'Connected Belonging' Approach expands these four key aspects, including the applied (competencies), resources (opportunities), psychological (motivation) and experiential (perceptions) in emphasising that while belonging might be felt individualistically (i.e., through perceptions and motivations), it is nonetheless experienced relationally (i.e., through opportunities and the resources generated), which can provide tangible skills and benefits for the individual (e.g., competencies).

The approach links 'individual identity' to:

- School identity
- Cultural and group identity
- Local community identity
- Place attachment
- Social identity
- Peer group identity
- Citizenship identity

According to Brown et al.:

> a school's role in wellbeing promotion therefore involves exploring children's sense of connection and identification with others, as well as what makes them unique as an individual. This involves strengthening students' sense of connection within the seven key domains of their lives, as well as the opportunity to build and affirm their individual identities. (Brown et al., 2025)

They go on to define the seven domains of the Connected Belonging framework below:

1. School identity refers both to the student's identity as a learner at the school and their sense of belonging as a member of the school community.

2. Cultural identity describes the part of an individual's sense of self that relates to their home background and culture(s).
3. Local community identity equates to children's sense of being valued, connected members of their local communities.
4. Place attachment recognises that individuals don't just form connections to people, but rather a sense of belonging is contextual – we feel belonging in relation to specific spaces that are meaningful to us.
5. Social identity relates to our intersectional identities, or how our identities arise from belonging to multiple social groups.
6. Peer group identity refers to children's connectedness to friends and peers, identified as a critical component in children's sense of school belonging.
7. Citizenship identity acknowledges children's and young people's sense of being both national and global citizens of a diverse, multicultural society.

> *'We find that students' perceptions of belonging are related to their individual characteristics, the school environment, and their perspectives on the broader social context.'*
> Allen (2025: 22)

DIVERSITY WALK

When I am working with staff during an INSET, I sometimes invite them to do a diversity walk around their school. This is a way of re-experiencing and re-imagining spaces that we might take for granted and often don't fully take in.

People describe empathy as walking in someone else's shoes – we need to be careful using that analogy for this exercise as I am never going to know what it feels like to be Black, Muslim or dyslexic, as they are not part of my identity. However, I can consider how it might feel to view the school through someone else's lens. Even better – I could do the walk with a diverse group of colleagues or students and ask them to share their thoughts.

Start by picking a protected characteristic which is not part of your lived experience. For this example, I will think about having a physical disability and being a wheelchair user. I will then spend some time walking around the school and considering it from that lens. Some questions to consider:

- How would I get access to the site? Are there any steps to navigate?
- How would I get access into the building? Is there a ramp and a door that opens for me?
- Which toilets and changing rooms would I use?
- How do I get upstairs? Is there a lift?
- In my favourite subject, which desk do I sit at and is it an accessible desk positioned somewhere I can readily access?
- Do I see myself represented in the curriculum for this subject?
- In the library, can I find any books written by or centring someone who looks like me?
- If there was a fire, how would I get out of the building?
- When I take in the corridor displays, do I see myself positively represented? (And is the lovely display for PE about Paralympians at my eye-level so I can see it?)
- At break time and for extra-curricular activities, which are accessible to me as a wheelchair user?

If you received an email this week saying you have a new student joining your group next week who holds this identity, what could you do proactively to make them feel included and support their sense of belonging before they arrive?

CASE STUDY 4.1

Ensuring all identities are represented

I was reviewing the DEIB practices and policies of a Midlands primary school. As we walked around the school, I saw an array of displays celebrating the diversity of their school, artwork capturing the identities of their community. Then we went into classrooms. In Year 5, there were two classes. In one was a boy in a wheelchair, in the other a brown girl wearing a Hijab. As I moved around the classrooms, taking in their learning journey on the walls, in their books and seeing the reading for pleasure books on offer, I noted an absence. I could not see either identity represented. When I debriefed the Deputy Headteacher later, she was mortified, but she thanked me for identifying the gap. She emailed me a week later to say she had ordered new books for the library and reading corners, and she had delivered an assembly to Year 5 where she had read them *The Proudest Blue* by Ibtihaj Muhammad and S.K. Ali. More importantly, the pupil had sat a bit taller and smiled at her brightly at the end of the assembly.

SAFE SPACES

Another exercise I regularly use in my training is asking people to traffic light or RAG-rate (traffic lighting using red/amber/green) the different spaces in a school to consider how safe and inclusive they made them feel.

Pick a time in your own educational journey and focus on a school setting you attended. Review the following list of common school spaces and reflect on how each one affirmed or eroded or had no impact on your identity at that time in your life (RAG-rate them). Feel free to add other spaces to the list.

How was your sense of belonging in each of these spaces?

- Playground
- Corridor
- Toilets
- Changing rooms
- Dining hall
- Classroom
- Tutor room
- Assembly hall
- Library
- Curriculum
- School bus
- After-school clubs

Find a trusted colleague and ask them to do the same thing, then compare notes. Get curious about the spaces that affirmed you and challenged them, and vice versa. Talk out some of your key memories from being a pupil and how these spaces made you feel.

Consider doing this with a group of pupils and listen to/learn from them. Do not assume that your needs for belonging as a pupil is what they need to belong. We often overthink and overcomplicate it. Asking people what they need to belong is a great starting point.

THE GEC'S 26,000 VOICES REPORT

Dr Nic Ponsford, founder of the Global Equality Collective (GEC), has spent the last few years collating data about staff and students' experiences of school life. Here are some key findings from their research into how safe, seen or supported young people feel in school (Global Equality Collective, 2025):

- 64% of students say they don't feel safe at school.
- 30% of students from single-parent families have missed school due to safety concerns.

- 18% of students with mental health needs feel supported to achieve.
- 33% of students with invisible disabilities say their needs are not understood in class.
- 21% of LGBTQ+ students feel their gender identity is respected.

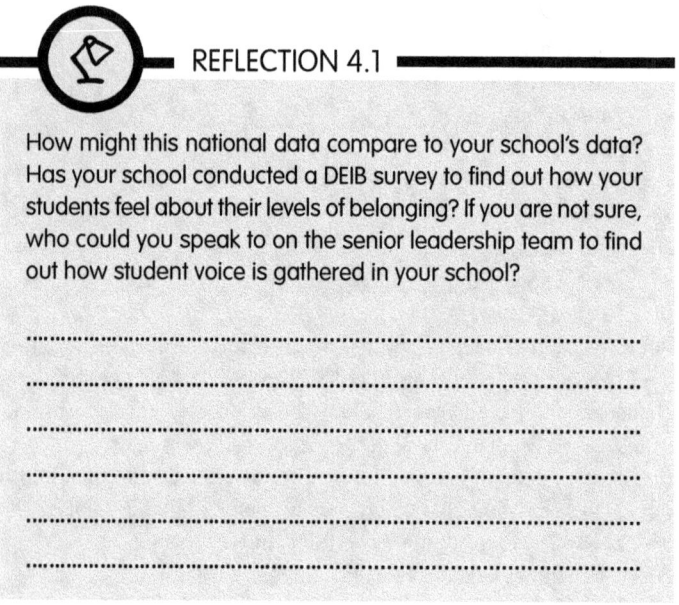

REFLECTION 4.1

How might this national data compare to your school's data? Has your school conducted a DEIB survey to find out how your students feel about their levels of belonging? If you are not sure, who could you speak to on the senior leadership team to find out how student voice is gathered in your school?

....
....
....
....
....
....

DON'T OVERTHINK IT!

I often get asked by DEIB leaders to support them in analysing their student survey data as they are overwhelmed. And to be quite honest, I am when I see they have asked 50+ open questions to hundreds of students.

Keep it simple, less is more. See a DEIB survey or focus group as a pulse-check, keep it to no more than ten questions and then follow up later based on what you find out from phase 1 of your enquiry.

Some things to consider:

- What are the pros and cons of a named survey?
- What is useful about closed questions?
- How might open questions help me understand more?
- How can I make sure that the survey is accessible to all learners?

> *'Being an effective teacher means ensuring all students are included and feel a sense of belonging in the classroom.'*
> Yamina Bibi (2024: 34)

IDENTITY-AFFIRMING CLASSROOMS

Kwame Sarfo-Mensah, author of *Learning to Relearn: Supporting Identity in a Culturally Affirming Classroom* (Sarfo-Mensah, 2024) challenges his readers to consider how to make their classroom feel like home for their pupils.

REFLECTION 4.2

What do you associate with home? How does home make you feel? How can you carry some of these associations and feelings through to your learning environment?

....
....

(Continued)

He defines home as spaces where we:

- Feel a sense of psychological and emotional safety and comfort
- Can express ourselves unapologetically
- Receive support and care from loved ones
- Belong and feel welcomed, valued and accepted
- Thrive off routine and stability
- Are connecting intimately with our loved ones
- Hold cherished memories and family history near and dear to our hearts

How does his definition of home compare to yours?

MIRRORS, WINDOWS AND SLIDING DOORS

The metaphor of mirrors, windows and sliding doors offers a powerful framework for curriculum development. This metaphor, introduced by Dr Rudine Sims Bishops (Bishop, 1990) encapsulates the essence of diversity, equity, inclusion and belonging within educational contexts, emphasising the importance of reflection, observation and engagement for all learners.

Mirrors in the curriculum are essential for students to see themselves – their cultures, identities and experiences – reflected in what they learn. When students encounter stories, histories and perspectives that resonate with their own lives, they feel validated and recognised. For curriculum specialists and subject leaders, this means incorporating diverse voices and narratives across all subjects. For example, in literature, selecting texts from a variety of authors who represent different backgrounds.

Windows offer students a view into the lives and experiences of people different from themselves. Through these glimpses, students develop empathy, understanding and a broader perspective of the world. Windows help dismantle stereotypes and prejudices, fostering a more inclusive mindset. To create these windows, educators need to curate a curriculum that includes global perspectives and diverse narratives. For example, in geography, this might involve studying various cultures and their relationships with the environment.

Sliding doors represent opportunities for students to enter into, and interact with, different worlds. This element encourages active engagement and personal reflection. When students can metaphorically 'step into' the experiences of others, they gain deeper insights of different identities and build meaningful connections. Interactive projects, collaborative learning experiences and role-playing activities serve as sliding doors in the curriculum. For instance, a history project where students re-enact historical events from multiple perspectives.

To integrate these concepts effectively, curriculum specialists and subject leaders must be intentional and thoughtful in their approach. This involves:

- **Reviewing and revising existing curriculum**: Conducting thorough audits to identify gaps and biases. Ensuring that the content reflects a diverse range of voices and perspectives.
- **Collaborating with diverse communities**: Engaging with parents/carers, community leaders and organisations to

gather input and resources. This collaboration can enrich the curriculum with authentic, representative materials.
- **Providing professional development**: Equipping teachers with the skills and knowledge to deliver an inclusive curriculum. Training on cultural competence, unconscious bias and inclusive teaching strategies.
- **Utilising technology and media**: Leveraging digital resources to access a wider array of content. Using online platforms, virtual exchanges and multimedia can bring diverse voices and experiences into the classroom.
- **Encouraging student voice and choice**: Empowering students to share their stories and choose projects that reflect their interests and identities. Designing a student-centred approach fosters a sense of ownership and relevance in their learning.

RESOURCES 4.1

Watch Dr Sims Bishops' talk: Mirrors, Windows and Sliding Glass Doors www.youtube.com/watch?v=_AAu58SNSyc

To find out more about how to diversify your curriculum I recommend reading Bennie Kara's work. *Diversity in Schools* (2020) is full of little gems to get started. *The Diverse Curriculum* (2024) is a longer read and breaks down the research and subject-specific approaches.

IDEAS FOR YOUR CLASSROOM

What are the things we can proactively do to design inclusion into the space?

We can:

- Pronounce student names correctly
- Use correct gender pronouns for students
- Understand that social emotional learning must be built into our practice
- Plan lessons and employ teaching techniques that are neuroinclusive
- Make our classrooms accessible to students with physical disabilities
- Foster a language-rich environment, encouraging oral language practice, and building on students' home languages
- Adopt a restorative approach to behaviour management and relationship building
- Commit to embedding anti-bias approaches and an anti-racist lens to our teaching

REFLECTION 4.3

How many of these inclusive teaching approaches do you already have in your teacher's toolkit? Which do you think about more carefully? How might this positively impact your learners?

....
....
....
....
....
....

SPOTLIGHT ON GOOD PRACTICE

No Outsiders – a national charity with a vision for inclusive education that promotes community cohesion to prepare young people and adults for life as global citizens in modern Britain. https://no-outsiders.com/

The Black Curriculum – a national charity. The Black Curriculum invites us to re-imagine the future of education through Black British history. Their vision is to empower all students (3–25) with a sense of national and cultural identity and belonging through the teaching of Black British history. https://theblackcurriculum.com/

# NOTE IT DOWN

We have covered a lot in Chapter 4. Gather your thoughts, next steps and takeaways here:

Make a list of any new terms, concepts and acronyms you want to come back to as you grow your DEIB vocabulary bank:

CHAPTER 5
CALL TO ACTION: WHAT DO WE DO NEXT?

What are YOU going to do next?

> *'Education is the most powerful weapon which you can use to change the world.'*
> *Nelson Mandela (cited in Ratcliffe, 2017)*

Remember…

You have the purpose, you have the passion, you have the positionality, the privilege and the power to make a difference.

YOUR SPHERE OF INFLUENCE

We each have an influence over the people around us – the children we teach, the colleagues we collaborate with, the teams we lead, the schools we govern, the families we support, the communities we serve, the profession we belong to.

BE AN ALLY

> **Allies:** noun. A state formally cooperating with another for a military or other purpose.
>
> Verb. Combine or unite a resource or commodity with (another) for mutual benefit.
>
> **Allyship:** A lifelong process of building relationships based on trust, consistency and accountability with marginalised individuals and/or groups of people. Not self-defined – work and efforts must be recognised by those you are seeking to ally with.

Why do we all need to be Inclusive Allies?

- We are all humans.
- We are all equal.
- We all need to check our privilege.

- We need to empathise with the struggle that some people go through.
- We need to be aware of the obstacles and the barriers in the way of some people on their journey.
- We need to be aware of the impact of prejudice and discrimination.

Allyship is a process and everyone has more to learn. Allyship involves a lot of listening. Sometimes, people say 'doing ally work' or 'acting in solidarity with' to reference the fact that 'ally' is not an identity, it is an ongoing and lifelong process that involves a lot of work.

Inclusive Allyship is:

- Men working alongside women to smash glass ceilings and advance gender equality.
- White people working alongside people of colour to smash concrete ceilings and advance racial equity.
- Heterosexual people working alongside Lesbian, Gay, Bisexual, Transgender, Queer and Intersex people to smash the gay glass ceiling.
- Able-bodied people working alongside disabled people to smash the disability glass ceiling. Allyship is about confronting othering, 'isms', privilege and prejudice. Allyship is about standing up and speaking out on social justice issues.

CHALLENGE DEROGATORY LANGUAGE

What we say has an impact on the people around us, whether it is about them or about someone they know who holds that identity, exclusionary language causes harm to the individual and collective identity. We often hear things being said that are inappropriate – throwaway comments, jokes and stereotyping feed into the problem and challenge someone's sense of belonging.

DISRUPT MICROAGGRESSIONS

Harmful language quickly becomes harmful behaviour. A microaggression is a statement, action or incident regarded as an instance of indirect, subtle or unintentional discrimination against members of a marginalised group such as a racial or ethnic minority.

The everyday verbal, nonverbal and environmental slights, snubs or insults – whether intentional or unintentional – that communicate hostile, derogatory or negative messages to individuals based solely upon their marginalised group membership. Microaggressions repeat or affirm stereotypes about a minority group, and they tend to minimise the existence of discrimination or bias, intentional or not.

Zahara Chowdhury (2025) states: 'It's hard to put into words what many of us—especially those who are "othered"—are carrying right now. When I speak to friends and colleagues, the feelings range from sadness and fear to resilience, resistance, and even indifference. For me, the world feels both tragic and surreal. I'm tired and frustrated'. We often witness people being excluded and othered, but we do nothing. Our passivity thus makes us complicit and part of the problem.

RESOURCES 5.1

Watch Meena Ayittey's short film: Badlands, All the Little Things
www.shots.net/news/view/new-film-cuts-to-the-heart-of-racist-micro-aggressions

CALL IT OUT, IN AND ON

We all need to be empowered to challenge it when we hear it and when we see it. Some tips – getting curious, sharing some knowledge or encouraging some empathy are three ways to disarm someone who is using clumsy and damaging language.

- 'Calling it out' – we do it publicly in the classroom, in the meeting room, to stop it in the moment before someone is harmed.
- 'Calling it in' – we do it privately at a later stage, probably in a one to one.
- 'Calling it on' – is one I have only heard used recently but we do it in a way of holding people to account and expecting better.

A CALL TO ACTION

Being an Inclusive Ally is about everyone being conscious of our own identity and lived experience, but being equally aware of our gaps in understanding and where we hold privilege. We need to do the work, the inner work, to reflect, to learn and to grow, in order to be able to do the outer work where we show up, stand up and speak out.

Allyship will not always be comfortable. We need to get comfortable with being uncomfortable. We need to check our privilege and realise that our momentary discomfort is not comparable to the long-term discomfort that people live with. Trauma and tragedy are the lived experiences for many people.

Becoming and being an Inclusive Ally requires intention, commitment and action. We need to lean into this space, no matter how hard, how painful and how uncomfortable it is.

For teachers and those working in education we need to consider the impact we can have in our classrooms and our schools. We need to be the change in teaching acceptance. We need to celebrate diversity and create a sense of belonging for all identities. We need to ensure that our environments are physically and psychologically safe for everybody. We need to have the big conversations about the world to equip everybody with the knowledge, skills and values to navigate society.

Even the most inclusive leaders admit they have room to grow. The work never stops, yet it is your choice to start, to practise and to be better every single day. If you search our website for 'allyship', a series of blogs and resources will come up, including our DEIB toolkit on this theme.

RESOURCES 5.2

Watch Adrian McLean's TED Talk: Inclusive Allyship www.youtube.com/watch?v=-krLTF1e9v8&list=PL5Qv_qeF-NpUqXBsVB9KHAhJVcBeWlfFq&index=1&t=330s

IDEAS FOR THE CLASSROOM

'Embracing allyship means more than just supporting others in theory; it means taking concrete actions to stand up against injustice.'
Frances Akinde (2024: 24)

SUSTAINABLE DEVELOPMENT GOALS

The 2030 Agenda for Sustainable Development, adopted by all United Nations Member States in 2015, provides a shared blueprint for peace and prosperity for people and the planet, now and into the future. At its heart are the 17 Sustainable Development Goals (SDGs), which are an urgent call for action by all countries – developed and developing – in a global partnership. At least seven of the UN's SDGs speak to DEIB.

STRATEGIC INTENT

Cultivating a culture of belonging starts with strategic intent, is developed through explicit communication of the commitment and is strengthened by a shared responsibility and a collective endeavour.

A marginal gains approach to incremental changes can create a ripple effect through every aspect of school life.

Here are ten areas to explore:

1. Inclusive leadership
2. Inclusive language
3. Inclusive behaviour
4. Inclusive policies
5. Inclusive practices
6. Inclusive curriculum
7. Inclusive communities
8. Inclusive spaces
9. Inclusive meetings
10. Inclusive recruitment

I am going to end with a case study. Over the past five years, whilst doing this work full-time, we have worked with staff across thousands of schools and hundreds of trusts. Inclusive Multi Academy Trust is a small group of primary schools in Watford who have really invested in the work. In 2025, they were nominated for the TES small MAT of the year and also for the MAT Excellence EDI Award. This is an extract from my endorsement for their nominations:

CASE STUDY 5.1

An authentic commitment

The Belonging Effect (formerly known as Diverse Educators) team have been delighted to collaborate with the Inclusive MAT for the last few years to support their whole school community: we have delivered DEIB training for them on INSET days; we have worked with their governors and trustees on their DEIB strategy; we have supported their Executive team and headteachers in

(Continued)

shaping their DEIB vision; we have delivered pupil assemblies and workshops; we have contributed to their DEIB offer for all of their community stakeholders.

They are values-led in their leadership, they have an authentic commitment to inclusion, for all of their community, for all identities, and they are committed to identifying barriers, reducing marginalisation and challenging inequities. Their DEIB commitment is a golden thread throughout their external partnerships, and they often invite friendly collaborators to join our sessions, to generously share their investment and to consciously expand their sphere of influence in their region.

It has been great to see them stepping out of their comfort zones to attend events such as Racial Equity Networking Dinners (REND) to develop their consciousness around some of the more complex issues impacting their trust and wider community such as racialised identities. As a team of leaders, they are very willing to be vulnerable and to share their challenges to learn and grow on their journeys as individuals and as a team. Inclusive MAT are truly at the heart of their community and are a beacon of hope for the impact that schools can have in ensuring that all stakeholders belong and thrive.

REFERENCES

Ahmed, N. (2024) 'Do you feel like you belong at work? Here's why it's so important for your health, happiness and productivity' in *The Conversation*. Available at: https://theconversation.com/do-you-feel-like-you-belong-at-work-heres-why-its-so-important-for-your-health-happiness-and-productivity-226335

Akinde, F. (2024) *Be An Ally, Not a Bystander*. London: Sage.

Allen, K-A. (2020) *The Psychology of Belonging*. London: Routledge.

Allen. K.A. (2025) 'School belonging: evidence, experts, and everyday gaps', *Educational Psychology Review*, 37(84).

Allen, K-A., Kern, M.L., Rozek, C.S, McInerny, D.M. and Slavic, G.M. (2021) 'Belonging: A review of conceptual issues, an integrative framework, and directions for future research'. *Australian Journal of Psychology*, 73(1), pp. 87–102.

Angelou, M. (1987) *All God's Children Need Travelling Shoes*. Virago.

Bibi, Y. (2024) *A Little Guide for Teachers: Thriving in Your First Years of Teaching*. London: Sage.

Bishop R.S. (1990) 'Mirrors, windows, and sliding glass doors'. *Perspectives*, 6(3), pp. ix–xi.

Brett, A and Brassington, J. (2023) *Pride and Progress: Making LGBT+ Inclusive Spaces*. London: Corwin.

Brown, B. (2012) *Daring Greatly*. New York: Gotham Books.

Brown, C., Douthwaite, A., Donnelly, M. and Shay, M. (2025) 'Connected Belonging: A relational and identity-based approach to schools' role in promoting child wellbeing', *British Educational Research Journal*, 51(4): 1927–1965.

Chowdhury, Z. (2025) *Creating Belonging in the Classroom: A practical guide to having brave and difficult conversations*. London: Bloomsbury.

Crenshaw, K. (1989) 'Demarginalizing the intersection of race and sex: A black feminist critique of antidiscrimination doctrine, feminist theory and antiracist politics'. *University of Chicago Legal Forum*, 1989(8).

Duckworth, S. (2020) *Wheel of Power and Privilege*. Available at: https://www.researchgate.net/figure/Wheel-of-Power-Privilege-and-Marginalization-by-Sylvia-Duckworth-Used-by-permission_fig1_364109273 (accessed 13 October 2025).

Eastwood, O. (2022) *Belonging: Unlock Your Potential with the Ancient Code of Togetherness*. London: Quercus.

Edmondson, A.C. (2018) *The Fearless Organization: Creating Psychological Safety in the Workplace for Learning, Innovation, and Growth*. New Jersey: John Wiley & Sons.

Edurio (2021) *Equality, Diversity and Inclusion (EDI) Review*. Available at: https://home.edurio.com/resources/insights/edi-report/ (accessed 13 October 2025).

Equality Act 2010. Available at: www.legislation.gov.uk/ukpga/2010/15/contents (accessed 3 September 2025).

Fenwick, T. and Sanders, S. (2012) Educating out prejudice–focusing on homophobia and transphobia. *Race Equality Teaching*, 30(2).

Fosslien, L. and West Duffy, M. (2019) *No Hard Feelings: The Secret Power of Embracing Emotions at Work*. Portfolio.

Global Equality Collective (2025) *26,000 Voices: What Students and Staff Really Think About Inclusion*. Available at: https://www.thegec.education (accessed 4 November 2025).

Hagerty, B.M. and Patusky, K. (1995) 'Developing a measure of sense of belonging'. *Nursing Research*, 44(1), pp. 9–13.

Kaback, S. (2025) 'Belonging in a school community'. *Choice Literacy*. Available at: https://choiceliteracy.com/article/belonging-in-a-school-community (accessed 13 October 2025).

Kara, B. (2020) *A Little Guide for Teachers: Diversity in Schools*. London: Sage.

Kara, B. (2024) *The Diverse Curriculum*. London: Sage.

Lash, J.P. (1980) *Helen and Teacher: The Story of Helen Keller and Anne Sullivan Macy*. Delacorte Press.

LinkedIn Talent Solutions (2016) *The Power of Belonging: Pat Wadors Talent Connect 2016* [Video]. YouTube. Available at: https://www.youtube.com/watch?v=xwadscBnlhU (accessed 13 October 2025).

Livermore, D. (2009) *Cultural Intelligence*. Michigan: Baker Academic.

Maslow, A.H. (1943) 'A theory of human motivation'. *Psychological Review*, 50(4), pp. 370–96.

McIntosh, P. (2020) 'White privilege: Unpacking the invisible knapsack', in *Gender, Race & Canadian Law: A Custom Textbook*. Fernwood Publishing, p. 92.

Muhammad, I. (2019) *The Proudest Blue: A Story of Hijab and Family*. Boston: Little Brown.

Myatt, M. (2017) *Walking the Talk*. Available at: www.marymyatt.com/blog/2017-12-09/walking-the-talk (accessed 8 January 2019).

National Foundation for Educational Research (NFER) (2024) 'Ethnic diversity in the teaching workforce: evidence review'. Available at: https://www.nfer.ac.uk/publications/ethnic-diversity-in-the-teaching-workforce-evidence-review/ (accessed 13 October 2025).

National Foundation for Educational Research (NFER) (2025) 'National Foundation for Educational Research'. Available at: https://www.nfer.ac.uk/publications/ethnic-disparities-in-entry-to-teacher-training-teacher-retention-and-progression-to-leadership/ (accessed 13 October 2025).

Office of National Statistics (ONS) (2021) *Census 2021*. Available at: www.ons.gov.uk/census

Ratcliffe, S. (2017) *Oxford Essential Quotations*. Oxford University Press. Available at: https://www.oxfordreference.com/display/10.1093/acref/9780191843730.001.0001/q-oro-ed5-00007046 (accessed 3 November 2025).

Sarfo-M.K. (2024) *Learning to Relearn: Supporting Identity in a Culturally Affirming Classroom*. London: Routledge.

Scott, K. (2017) *Radical Candor*. London: Macmillan.

Scott, S. (2017) *Fierce Conversations: Achieving Success in Work and in Life, One Conversation at a Time*. London: Piatkus.

Sinek, S. (2011) *Start with Why: How Great Leaders Inspire Everyone to Take Action*. London: Penguin.

Sollis, B. (2014) 'Community is much more than belonging to something; it's about doing something together that makes belonging matter'. Available at: https://briansolis.com/2014/12/community-much-belonging-something-something-together-makes-belonging-matter (accessed 24 October 2025).

Stones, S. and Glazzard, J. (2019) 'The experiences of teachers who identify as lesbian, gay, bisexual, transgender or queer (LGBTQ+)'. BERA. Available at: https://www.bera.ac.uk/blog/the-experiences-of-teachers-who-identify-as-lesbian-gay-bisexual-transgender-or-queer-lgbtq (accessed 13 October 2025).

Syed, M. (2019) *Rebel Ideas*. London: John Murray Publishers Ltd.

The New Britain Project (2024) 'Missing Mothers'. Available at: https://www.newbritain.org.uk/missing-mothers (accessed 13 October 2025).

Wilson, H. and Kara, B. (2022) *Diverse Educators: A Manifesto*. University of Buckingham Press.

INDEX

acceptance, 13, 85
accomplices, 5
Adverse Childhood
    Experiences, 14
advocates, 5
age, 14, 16
allies, 5, 82
allyship, 82, 83, 85, 86
Angelou, Maya, 28

belief, 29, 33, 40
belonging, 8, 11–14, 27, 46–48,
    57–58, 64–68
bias, 75, 76, 84
Brassington, Jo, 47
Brett, Adam, 47
British Values, 33–34
Brown, Brené, 39, 46
Burke-Harris, Nadine, 14

census, 19–20, 49
change, 5, 27, 85, 86
Chowdhury, Zahara, 84
Citizens UK, 25
civil partnership, 14
classrooms, 47, 64–66, 73–74,
    76–77, 86
commitment, 8, 37, 85, 87–88
community, 4–5, 10, 13, 24–25,
    34–35, 54, 61, 75
Connected Belonging, 66–68
connection, 58, 67, 75
corridors, 69, 71

courageous conversations, 38–39
Crenshaw, Kimberlé, 17
crisis, 51
cultivating, 8, 86
Cultural Intelligence, 59
culture, 29–32, 37
curriculum, 34, 74–76, 78

DEIB, 1–8, 20, 35, 50, 54,
    57–59, 72
democracy, 33
disability, 14, 16, 23, 69, 77
discrimination, 14, 17–18, 35,
    50, 53, 84
Diverse Educators, 87
diversity, 6, 8, 18, 19, 24–25,
    28–29, 49, 64–66,
    68–69, 85
Duckworth, Sylvia, 20

education, 3, 5, 49, 82, 85
Edurio, 50, 51
emotional tax, 21
equalities objectives, 35
equalities policy, 34–38
equality, 6, 83
Equality Act, 14–15, 35
equity, 6, 8, 74
ethnic diversity, 19, 51
exclusion, 5

faith, 20, 33
feminism, 4

Floyd, George, 10
Fosslien, Liz, 54

gender identity, 16, 20, 72
gender reassignment, 14
Global Majority, 18–19
Golden Circle, 2–3
golden thread, 3, 88
governors, 5, 28, 36, 51, 87
grassroots, 5, 25
group think, 55–56

hate crimes, 23–24
HOPE not hate, 25

identity, 16–23, 47, 67–70, 73–74, 83
impact, 3, 28, 83
inclusion, 7, 8, 28–29
individual liberty, 33
intention, 28, 49, 85
intersectionality, 16–19

Kara, Bennie, 76

languages, 16, 19, 83
leaders, 5, 28, 37, 51, 54, 72, 75, 85
library, 42, 69, 71
lived experience, 16, 20, 22, 69, 85

margins/marginalised, 10, 12, 15, 20, 49, 50, 59, 82, 84
marriage, 14
Maslow, Abraham, 11
Maslow's Hierarchy, 11
maternity, 14
McIntosh, Peggy, 21
McLean, Adrian, 86
Meadows, Emily, 54

microaggressions, 84
Missing Mothers, 50
mission, 30–31, 37
Mission 44, 51–52
Multi-Academy Trust (MAT), 53, 59, 87–88
mutual respect, 33
Myers, Verna, 7

NFER, 50, 51–53

ONS, 19

pipeline, 54, 59
playgrounds, 39, 71
positionality, 5, 82
power, 4, 5, 20–22, 54, 56
pregnancy, 14
prejudice, 21, 23, 36, 53, 75, 83
privilege, 5, 17, 20–22, 82, 85
Protected Characteristics, 14, 15, 35, 36–37
psychological safety, 37, 40–41
Pupil Premium (PP), 4

race, 14, 16, 17, 23
rebel ideas, 55–56
recruitment, 50–52, 54, 55
religion, 14, 16, 20, 23
representation, 4–5, 50, 57, 61, 70
retention, 50–52, 58
rule of law, 33

safe spaces, 20, 70–71
safeguarding, 36
Sanders, Sue, 49
schools, 4–5, 11, 28–42, 46–49, 51, 54, 56, 67–72, 87–88
SEND, 19
sex, 14, 16
sexual orientation, 14, 16, 20, 23

sexuality, 20
Sinek, Simon, 2
social justice, 4, 5, 7, 17, 25, 83
society, 5, 11, 30, 34, 85
staffrooms, 46–47, 57
strategy, 17, 50, 51, 54, 59, 60, 86–87
support staff, 56
Syed, Matthew, 56

teachers, 4, 5, 28, 29, 47, 48, 52–53, 85
Thomas, Aisha, 25

tolerance, 33
trauma, 85

usualising, 49

values, 31–34
vision, 30–31, 37

Wadors, Pat, 58
WomenEd, 5, 49
workforce, 5, 48–49, 51–52

www.ingramcontent.com/pod-product-compliance
Lightning Source LLC
Chambersburg PA
CBHW071214070526
44584CB00019B/3027